Police Officers Prayer

Lord I ask for courage
Courage to face and Conquer my own fears...
Courage to take me Where others will not go...
I ask for strength
Strength of body to protect others And strength of spirit to
lead others...
I ask for dedication
Dedication to my job, to do it well. Dedication to my
community,
To keep it safe...

Give me Lord, concern
For others who trust me
And compassion for
those who need me...

And please Lord

Through it all
Be at my side...

Disclaimer

Contents

Foreword

Justice delayed, they say, is justice denied. My experience has taught me otherwise though. I have worked in Law Enforcement for a major part of my adult life. Moreover, I had passionately followed crime all my life. Chasing criminals and having them answer for their crimes was a way of life for me. Currently I teach Criminal Law and Own a Private Security Company. With so much experience at hand in Law Enforcement, and Teaching Criminal Law, I could say that some crimes see the light of the day after several years of their being committed. Not all that is "buried stays buried forever". Some acts return to haunt the guilty until they are brought to answer for their

Crimes.

This book is about one of the few most

engulfing cases, I had experienced during my

service as a Law Enforcement Officer. It is a

detailed recount of what happened to my friend

and fellow officer—Christopher Todd Horner. It

was in March of 1998, just before Dawn, that

Officer Horner was marched into a Cemetery

and Executed with his own Service Firearm. I

was working for The Haines City Police

Department, Haines City Florida, when I had to

go through the pain and trauma of losing a

good friend. His untimely death was not just a

loss to his family and our Department, but to

the community as a whole.

I want to shed light in this dark ending through this story, for it will teach you that 'truth sets us free.' This narrative will explain how one person's goodness can reform another person because Horner's good soul and his family's sympathy moved a criminal to the point of redemption.

Miracle, you say?

No, its fate!

I would also dwell deep in the technicalities of the case. The book contains detailed follow up on several petitions, hearings, arrests, and much more. There will be times when the reader would like to think that this is fiction but alas! This is the reality of the world we live in.

Read this tale to learn the truth about how

Officer Christopher Todd Horner died.

"The magic of a good soul never fades, even

after the spell of enchantment is long dead"

Darren W. Freeman

Chapter 1

The Death of Officer Christopher Horner (1998)

It was in March of 1998, when the Haines City Police Department had lost an Officer — Christopher Todd Horner! There was a report of a bank robbery and the Police in the area were on alert. The Holiday Inn branch in Dundee, Florida had been robbed and the police were on the lookout for the suspects. Officer Horner had just come on duty in the twilight hour before Dawn.

After his morning briefing Officer Horner started his patrol. He was doing a general Patrol of a small cemetery on the outskirts of the City.

He was a single person unit and drove into the Oakland Cemetery.

Now the cemetery was and still is considered an area of high crime, especially for leaving stolen vehicles and drug trafficking. This was enough to raise the suspicions of any police officer. As he drove in he spotted a suspicious vehicle parked off to the side. He drove around the cemetery and pulled his car behind the suspicious vehicle. He flashed the Spot Light of his car on the vehicle. He noticed what appeared to be several people sitting in an Oldsmobile.

Officer Horner radioed to Dispatch that he was out with a Suspicious Vehicle. He exited his vehicle drew his service weapon and ordered the occupants out of the vehicle. Officer Horner was still by himself and the Police Dispatch had not sent any assistance to him.

This was a group of people. Officer Horner had them exit their vehicle. Unbeknown to him there was another person. This person had walked off from the vehicle — Fowler, who had split up from them to use cocaine. Fowler watched Officer Horner drive into the Cemetery and hid behind some bushes just north of the Cemetery gravestones. He watched Officer Horner make contact with the rest of the group from the vehicle and crept up behind Officer Horner attacking him and wrestling his firearm from him. The other suspects all attacked

Officer Horner and held him to the ground. Officer Horner had referred to one of them by name, at which point Fowler told them that Horner had to go. They marched him into the center of the Cemetery forcing him to his knees. Fowler then shot him once in the head with Officer Horner's own Duty Firearm, causing his death. No one was sent to assist Officer Horner. It was after approximately25 minutes, and repeated radio calls to Officer Horner, that Officer Horner's Supervisor went to check on him, and discovered his body. The only information that was known at the time was what Officer Horner had originally radioed to his Dispatch.

Murder or suicide? — The speculations went

on

Sgt. Sandra Spicer was the shift supervisor when

this unfortunate incident occurred. She only

knew that Officer Horner was investigating a

suspicious vehicle without any visible license

plate, which was parked in Oakland Cemetery.

This was all the information she had and she

knew that criminals often abandoned stolen

cars at that place. She grew suspicious when

Horner did not return their calls and thus drove

over to the Cemetery.

She found Officer Horner's dead body lying

there with his service weapon tucked under his

body. Emergency medical personnel were called

who declared him dead on the spot and the

medical examiner explained that the bullet had

entered from the left side of his head from

behind. Moreover, it was confirmed that the

killing bullet had been shot from Horner's

service weapon. All of this made a strong case

for suicide and a majority of the people

believed it to be just that. Yet, there continued

to be speculations of this being a murder too.

However, there was no evidence to make a

strong case.

Chapter 2

The Murder in the Cemetery

The investigations were moved to the Polk County Sherriff's Office and Homicide Detective, Deanna Pry was made the lead on the case. However, her superiors removed her from the case within a week because the fact that the Sherriff's office would not consider that the demised had committed suicide, had made her extremely angry. The suicide dilemma created a feud in the Sherriff's office and no progress was made on the case. The death of Office Horner remained a mystery until the year 2002.

It was in the spring of the said year when Christopher Gamble who was among the Principal Actors in Officer Horner's shooting, decided to open up on the subject. He had been given a 20-year sentence for a robbery case and according to the sources, his coming up to help with the murder investigation of Officer Horner was an attempt to have his sentence reduced. He had claimed to have a crucial piece of information concerning Officer Horner's murder. What happened after that is covered in detail in the following chapters.

Christopher Gamble turned out to be the first step in a long investigation that led to the final catching of all the suspects involved in the heinous crime. While there are different stories circulating about the real intention of

Christopher Gamble with some believing that

he had a change of heart and others claiming

that he was just a criminal like the rest of them,

his claim of possessing the most important

piece for this crime's puzzle was definitely true.

It was, after all, his confession that had

unraveled the mystery in the first place.

Chapter 3

He who allows oppression, shares the crime.

Desiderius Erasmus

Christopher Gamble — the first arrest (1999)

Concerning the murder of Officer Horner, the first solid evidence had come in the form of Christopher Gamble. This man was notorious for his robberies. In 1999, he was arrested for conducting an armed robbery in a liquor store. This time, there was no way for him to cheat justice and the court sentenced him for 20 years. Four years after his arrest, the man experienced a change of heart and decided to tell Law Enforcement officials about what had really happened to Officer Horner.

This confession was the game changer for the case. At first, the officials had their suspicions regarding whether this criminal was telling the truth or just making up things only to have his sentence reduced. However, when they listened to his story, the details he was giving were on point and only a person who was present during the murder would have known them. His confession established the fact that Officer Horner's death was not a case of suicide but it was a case of murder in cold blood.

When Gamble decided to make a Gamble —
the confession that changed everything

In 2002, Gamble decided to make a gamble
when he told the officials investigating the
death of Officer Garner that he was one of the
suspects responsible for Horner's murder. He
was 26 years old then and was a Florida state
prisoner. Detective Louis Giampavolo had
interviewed him. Giampavolo was a member of
the cold case unit of the Polk County Sherriff's
Office. After listening to the suspect, the officer
had decided to not file any formal state charges
as of yet because there were some
inconsistencies in the narration and the suspect
had admitted to allegedly lying to a Federal
Grand Jury in the past.

Yet there were some points that were rather strong and could not be ignored. Gamble stated that he had committed a robbery at the Holiday Inn. He had further admitted to committing the crime at gunpoint. His accomplices in the robbery included Andre Paige, Jeffrey Bouyie. Another man, and Fowler had conducted a separate robbery and had also stolen an Oldsmobile. The four of them plus another conspirator were to meet at the Cemetery for committing another crime that had been planned. However, their plans were disturbed by the arrival of Officer Horner. Their stolen car and black clothes were suspicious enough to catch the attention of any passersby and there was no way for them to get away from the situation without giving themselves up.

However, fortunately for them, one of their friends — Fowler — had left them for a while, presumably to use cocaine. The Haines City Police Officer had cornered them when Fowler was not with them. He had already reported to the station that he was investigating a suspicious vehicle. However, when Fowler returned from the Orange Grove, the officer was caught by surprise and before he could even know, Fowler attacked him from behind. His service weapon, a 9mm gun was snatched away from him.

At that moment, the officer addressed Gamble using his first name Chris. According to Gamble, the Officer's exact words were, "Chris, why are you doing this? Please do not do this." Horner had definitely identified Gamble from some previous robbery case. On hearing that the Rookie had recognized one of their gang members, the group panicked. As Gamble recalled, Fowler had said something along the line of "There is no way for us to walk away from this now" since the officer knew Gamble. That was when their other accomplice, Bouyie shouted, "Kill that cracker."

To Gamble's utter shock, Fowler obliged and pulled the trigger of Horner's gun. He had shot him at the back of his head behind his left ear.

Gamble decided to put the weapon under Horner's dead body in order to give the impression of suicide.

Gamble was now ready to offer all possible help to the authorities in catching the others. There was Andre Paige and Robert Winston to be tackled before they could move over to Fowler. The police officials decided to go quietly about the business. Gamble was to skip the death sentence in return for his help. He was ready to give evidence against Fowler in the court as well if the need arose.

Many people believe that Gamble had a change of heart and it was a yearning for redemption that led him to cooperate even at the risk of losing his life. They say that remorse can change even the hardest of men. Whether there is any truth in this or not might never be revealed but Gamble is definitely a strong protagonist of this story.

"The man who has a conscience suffers whilst acknowledging his sin. That is his punishment."
— Fyodor Dostoyevsky, Crime and Punishment

Law Enforcement Officers behind the Successful investigation of the Horner Murder Case

Chief W. J. Martin

Lieutenant J. Britt Williams

Major Joe Halman

Lieutenant Brian Rall

Sergeant Julio Lima

Sergeant Deborah Hamilton

Sergeant Michael Reckart

Sergeant Raymond Swilley

Detective Louis Giampavolo

Laurie Ward, Crime Scene Administrator

Lynda Raczynski, Crime Scene Technician

Nancy Shipman, Crime Scene Technician

Susan Deese, Crime Scene Technician

Chapter 4

Andre Paige — the second arrest (2004)

It is the highest form of self-respect to admit our errors and mistakes and make amends for them. To make a mistake is only an error in judgment, but to adhere to it when it is discovered shows infirmity of character.

Dale Turner

The credit should be given to the law enforcement Agency for tackling the case and investigation in the best possible way. Instead of making it public that they were looking for such and such suspects, they decided to work in private. This led to their successfully arresting the second suspect.

The next arrest in the case was of Andre Paige. He was a major narcotics dealer who had worked most of his life in close association with another notorious criminal, Bartolome Moya. In March 1998, he had been charged with a number of crimes, which mainly included robberies at Shoney's restaurant and a Florida Holiday Inn.

His name came up in the Horner murder case, when Gamble revealed it in his confession. At that time, the Law Enforcement Investigators were not entirely convinced of the confession being true. Therefore, instead of arresting the people named by Gamble, they decided to do some private investigation.

For this reason, Detective Louis Giampavolo — the Detective investigating the death case of Officer Christopher Horner, decided to interview Paige. It happened in March 2002 and according to the detective, it had been a simple interview without any arrest warrant, although Paige gave a different narration of the event later on. Moreover, he went on to file for his Miranda rights, stating that his statements from that interview should be suppressed because he was not provided with a Miranda Warning.

The district court believed that the testimony of the officers was more credible compared to the testimony provided by Paige about the events during the interview. Detective Giampavolo along with other officers who were present during that interview maintained that it was a non-custodial event, pertaining the issuing of the Miranda warnings invalid and unnecessary. The court agreed to it and thus denied the appeal made by Paige.

The Version provided by Detective Giampavolo

According to the story provided by the detective, Paige had actually agreed to get into the officer's car, which was an unmarked vehicle. He had accompanied the detective to the homicide Division office on his own consent without being forced at all. He had decided to go with the officer instead of coming on his own because he did not have a vehicle.

Chief Martin, who was at the office when they had arrived, testified that nothing in the manner the two had entered, suggested that this was an arrest, and backed this part of Detective Giampavolo's narration. Giampavolo further testified that he had clearly told Paige that he was not in custody or under arrest in any possible way. He had not handcuffed Paige either.

Further evidence that this was just an interview and not a serious interrogation that would have required the presence of Miranda warnings is that it had not even taken place in a locked cell and two other officers were present during the interview as well. The detective had then explained to Paige that his previous crime partner Christopher Gamble had made a confession concerning several robberies as well as his involvement with Officer Horner's death. Moreover, he told him that Gamble had also told other names among which, one name was Paige's.

According to the narration of the events provided by Detective Giampavolo, this had made Paige a little agitated and he had asked the officer to bring Gamble in and to ask him to say that to his face. The Detective had done that and Gamble was called. Christopher

Gamble informed Paige that he had told "everything" to the police.

After a while, Paige agreed that he was a part of the robbery they had committed at the Holiday Inn with their other accomplice, Bouyie. After that, the Detective allowed Paige to use the rest room unattended. Since the interview had ended and since Paige had no means to get to his home, Detective Giampavolo even gave him a lift to his girlfriend's house.

The Version provided by Paige

As per the narration provided by Paige though, he was taken to the homicide division forcefully with Detective Giampavolo telling him that he "needed" to come with them. He was sure that he had no other choice but to go with the officer.

Similarly, Paige claimed that the detective had accompanied him to the bathroom as well and thus, he believed it to be an interrogation as if he was under arrest. Moreover, according to him, the questions and answers session had taken place in a small cell. It was locked and the interview had lasted from 10 to 15 minutes.

Paige also said that Detective Giampavolo had told him that there was no need for him to worry about anything if he was ready to cooperate with the authorities. He further said that he had not asked for Gamble as claimed by the Detective but they had brought him there on their own. He further denied to admitting to be a part of any robbery.

His narration clearly indicated that he should have been given a Miranda Warning, as the law requires the authorities to provide them, if there is any restraint on the person's freedom of movement of a degree that would be associated with any formal arrest. This becomes crucial even if they have not been arrested.

What does the Court have to say about it? According to the law, a suspect is considered to be under arrest when a reasonable person is in the suspect's position and feels a sufficient level of restraint on their freedom of movement that is characterized associated to a formal arrest to the extent that he does not feel free to leave.

However, this criterion is defined from the perspective of a reasonable and innocent man. Therefore, even if Paige had felt that his freedom was restrained, it had nothing to do with how the law had been conducted since he was allowed to visit the Restroom, was sitting in a room that was not locked, and he was told by the Detective he could leave as well.

While it was acknowledged by the court that Paige had felt as if he was not free to leave the meeting or interrogation as he considered it a sort of arrest, his testimony had been of less credibility than the statement provided by the detective. Detectives are fact finders who are supposed to observe the statement personally and are in a better position to access the credibility of any statement. This means that the evidence must be accepted unless it defies the laws of nature and/or are contrary to common sense.

As the detective had driven Paige to his girlfriend's house, he was definitely not under arrest nor were his movements restricted. This means that this interview was not a custodial interrogation by any means. Therefore, the absence of Miranda warnings was appropriate and there was no need to suppress the statements that were made in that interview by Paige.

The Arrest of Paige

Paige was arrested in the September of 2002. At the time of the arrest, Detective Giampavolo testified about having advised Paige concerning his Miranda rights and he further added that Paige had said that he understood them.

Initially Paige claimed that he was not informed of any rights but later accepted that some kind of warnings might have been read to him.

Trial testimony as provided by Paige

The case of Officer Horner's death progressed slowly but it went into the right direction for sure. One by one, the knots tied around it loosened, until the whole case was resolved. Paige was one of the many important parts of the case. In fact, his testimony against Jeffrey Bouyie had been extremely crucial for solving the case.

Karen Meeks, who was his retained lawyer, represented him. In February of 2003, he testified against his partner Bouyie before the grand jury and then again, in May of 2003, during Jeffrey Bouyie's trial. Before making these statements, he should have asked for some kind of shield and should have proffered some kind of agreement or a plea to have his sentence reduced but strangely enough, this was not the case.

Later, he realized the mistake he had made and claimed that his lawyer's representation of his case during this time was inefficient to the point that he remained unrepresented during the case. He believed that the government had somehow violated him, making him give incriminating statements during the testimony. He also tried to use his older excuse in order to have his testimony suppressed, saying that he had not been presented with his Miranda rights before he was asked for his statements.

Despite his incessant accusations, the court remained of the opinion that there was no way his statements against Jeffrey Bouyie should be suppressed. He had made those statements as per the law and nobody had forcefully garnered the confessions out of him.

Sufficient Evidence

Paige's trial went by smoothly as there was sufficient evidence against him. To begin with, Christopher Gamble testified that he and his friends that included Paige, had robbed a hotel

namely a particular Holiday Inn. Their other
plan was to rob a branch of NationsBank. They
had gone to a cemetery in order to prepare and
plan for this bank robbery right before
daybreak. It was there that they had been
changing clothes and consuming drugs where
Officer Horner had cornered them. There were
masks, drugs, guns, and gloves inside their car,
which they had been using in their previous
missions. The Officer had approached them
there and he had known Christopher Gamble
already.

While Paige had not received any Miranda
warnings during his initial interview with the
detective, he had been informed about his
rights to remain silent during his arrest in

January and his trial in February. During the trial, the Judge informed him that if he made certain statements; they could be and would be used against him.

According to the statement given by Christopher Gamble, he had told the officer that he had come to the cemetery in order to visit his aunt. At that point, Officer Horner wanted to run down their names. This was when Charles Fowler had ambushed him. As a result of this situation, Officer Horner tried to scare them by using Christopher's first name. This led to a panicking situation among their group. All of them including Paige went a little crazy. They made Office Horner bend down on his knees and then Fowler aimed at the back of his head and shot him.

Andre T. Paige was 24 years old at the time of his arrest. He was charged with armed robbery, racketeering, and murder, as well as some other charges. He faced the death penalty as he was convicted as charged. While he had not shot Officer Horner, he had been involved in aiding and abetting another who had committed the actual murder.

The case went through several dramatic phases before coming to an end though. Paige's attorney Castillo, for example, tried to defame the testimony provided by Christopher Gamble. According to the lawyer, Gamble was a criminal and was ready to say and do anything just to have his sentence reduced.

Moreover, he emphasized that Gamble's theories had several inconsistencies, not to mention his unreliable character. He further emphasized that prosecutors were building up their side of the case on nothing but mud, for this is what Gamble's testimony really amounted to.

Gamble was supposed to face a sentence of around 107 years. However, his promise to cooperate with the authorities meant there were chances of reduction. Castillo thus built his case on this piece of information.

Moreover, he tried to use the fact in his favor that Jerry Hill, the State Attorney of Polk County had decided against charging anybody in this case. Castillo was adamant that Officer Horner had committed suicide, which was sad and most unfortunate but was not a valid reason to deprive other people of their lives.

However, Colonel Grady Judd from the Polk County's sheriff office could not see eye to eye with Castillo and the other people who were in favor of the suicide theory. He believed the suicide theory to be extremely erroneous. He had kept on emphasizing that ever since the death of the worthy Officer, the Law Enforcement Agency had been busy conducting a thorough and reliable investigation.

Therefore, he was positive that the confession made by Gamble was not the only thing providing evidence of this death being a murder and not a suicide.

He was quoted as saying that there are facts and figures that prove this case to be a murder. It does not hinge solely on the testimony of a single person. For example, there was always the evidence that Officer Horner was investigating a suspicious vehicle and the robberies that Gamble confessed to, had really happened. Moreover, he described the weapon with brilliant exactness, thus making it hard not to believe his version for only a person who was present there could have unraveled such details.

In 2002, Paige was indicted for the several robberies of which he had been a part. Other charges against him included being in possession of cocaine, resisting arrest on several occasions, and carrying firearms. However, he was exempted from facing the trial on the pretext of being mentally incompetent. His name coming up in the murder caused a major shift in that perspective.

Morris West, (prior to his removal from office for "Prostitution Charges"), was the Police Chief of Haines City and had considered the indictment of Paige as being a lucky discovery. The Police force and especially Officer Horner's colleagues had never forgotten their fallen comrade. They would often remember him, especially when patrolling around the vicinity of the cemetery. They had always kept hope alive..

Perhaps law enforcement officers have studied criminal minds for too long and are therefore adept at understanding their thinking process to the point of being able to predict their behaviors and their future course of action. This experience and expertise allows them to assess the situation to their advantage without breaking the law.

Moreover, many criminals are already feeling guilty for their crimes and if managed prudently, they could be persuaded into telling the truth. After all, the true aim of any law enforcement officer is to unravel the truth, ensuring their best that justice is served. Therefore, a good officer knows all such techniques and should use them too.

As a result of the deep confession, Paige was caught and justice was served to him. The criminal was charged with at least 10 counts. In addition to his involvement with Horner's murder, it included robbery and racketeering. His trial took place in September 2005 where the jury found him guilty. His sentence was life in prison along with a term of 60 years.

Let me be clear - no one is above the law. Not a politician, not a priest, not a criminal, not a police officer. We are all accountable for our actions.

— *Antonio Villaraigosa*

Did you know?

Homicide Detective Louis Giampavolo from Polk County Sheriff's office was included in the top choices in the Law Enforcement Officer of the Year award for 2004 by the Florida Retail Federation (FRF) for his impressive investigation skills, especially in the Officer Horner murder case.

The committee that selected him represented not just law enforcement but also represented the media, retail security, and the government. His supervisors had given his name due to the exemplary work he had showed in the Homicide Cold Case Squad. The homicide officer would work on the several unsolved death cases that kept coming up in the county. He would put extra effort and time to have them solved.

It was his aggressive approach at investigation that played a crucial role in finally solving the 6-year-old murder mystery of the Haines City Police Officer, Christopher Todd Horner. He was on the case for three years during which he traveled all over the US in order to follow up a huge number of leads. He succeeded in extracting a confession from one of the prime suspects. It was his pivotal investigation that resulted in the indictment of Christopher Gamble and Andre Paige — 2 major suspects in the murder case.

Chapter 5

Further advancement was made on the case with the third indictment, which turned out to be of Robert Earl Winston in September of 2006. He had not shot Officer Horner himself but he was arrested because he had aided and abetted another in doing so. Christopher Gamble had given his name in his testimony as well.

Robert Earl Winston was famous by his nickname "Pumpkin." At the time of his arrest, he was 26 years old and had already been involved in several robberies. He had already been incarcerated on an unrelated Polk County case at the Charlotte Correctional Institute. His involvement with the Horner case resulted in his two-count indictment.

In addition to being involved in the Officer Horner murder case, Robert Earl Winston, Jr. had also been charged for kidnapping, carjacking with a potentially deadly weapon, as well as aggravated battery by the detectives of Polk County Sheriff's Office. This charging had taken place on the 20th of September 2003. Haines City Police had been looking for him too.

In order to catch Winston, the authorities circulated the notification explaining that Winston is usually found around the Fuller Street area in Davenport. Moreover, they explained that he was known to frequently hang out with Charles Fowler — his cousin who had various warrants for his arrest as well. The suspect's mug shots were also attached along with it.

Winston was to be considered as "armed and dangerous" at that point and the public was directed to contact Polk County Sheriff's Office in case of any sighting. There was a cash reward in case a person's information led to the criminal's arrest even if the person chose to remain anonymous.

Convictions of Robert Earl Winston

Robert Earl Winston had been convicted for two reasons. In the legal terms, they were as follows:

1. Aiding and abetting another person who killed Haines City Police Officer Christopher Todd Horner with the motive to prevent him from communicating to any law enforcement officer information of the commission of a federal offence which was in violation of the 18U.S.C. §§ 1512(a)(1)(C) and (a)(3)(A), 1111, and 2

2. The second offence was aiding and abetting another who had knowingly carried and used a firearm in relation to the crime of violence, which had resulted in the murder of Officer Horner. This was in violation of 18U.S.C. §§ 924(c)(1)(A) and (j)(1), 1111, and 2.

Robert Earl Winston, however, had a plan of his own. He had a few charges to press against the police and a few appeals to make to the court.

Robert Earl Winston's Appeal

Winston believed that Brady v. Maryland, 83 S. Ct. 1194 (1963) had been violated by the government in his case. According to him, they should have disclosed a tacit agreement where the government had agreed to a considerable reduction in the witness's sentence in return for his cooperation in the investigation and provision of his truthful testimony.

The district reviewed his concern and concluded that there had been no violation of the said rule. According to Brady, the prosecution is under the obligation to inform the defense about the evidence that is favorable for the accused, that is if the evidence is material to punishment or guilt.

The real reason behind this disclosure in the legal terms is for ensuring that the jury is well aware of all the facts that would have motivated the witness to give the testimony. However, Winston had failed to bring concrete evidence that such an agreement existed either tacit or otherwise, between the witness and the Government that might not have been disclosed for the jury, either before or during his trial.

While it is true that the Government had extended favorable treatment to the witness, decent treatment from their side does not imply in any case that an agreement has been made between the two parties, which should be disclosed to the jury under Brady. Since Robert Earl Winston had failed to prove that he had in fact, made any kind of agreement with the Government, he had no right to file for a Brady violation.

The other appeal made by Winston was that the district court was in error in allowing a medical examiner to give a testimony on the basis of forensic reports that were provided by another examination. According to him, this was in violation with the Sixth Amendment. However, the court looked into this matter in detail, and it was clear that the second accusation was also invalid as well.

According to United States v. Steed,<u>548 F.3d961</u>, 975 (11th Cir. 2008), there is no harm in building an expert decision on a previous one if it is treated as concrete proof and is considered reliable in general. Thus, the district court has not erred when it had accepted the testimony of an expert witness who might have relied on some other expert's forensic report.

As long as the law was intact and not damaged, building evidence from a previous report was allowed.

As Winston Churchill had said, "The farther backward you can look the farther forward you will see."

The court case was thus closed and the convictions on Robert Earl Winston were proven to be true.

While there is no denying that facts and figures are of utmost importance when it comes to solving a case, especially one that is as sensitive as Office Horner's murder case was, there should always be some room left for imagination and emotions. Logic can only take you so far and sometimes solving of a case arequires the examination of feelings, putting you in the place of the dead or understanding how does a murderer operate.

James Reese once said, "There are certain clues at a crime scene which, by their very nature, do not lend themselves to being collected or examined. How does one collect love, rage, hatred, fear...? These are things that we're trained to look for."

A good detective finds facts but a great one looks beyond the facts. He tries to solve the case by taking into account all the possible angles of a situation. The team handling the case of Officer Horner turned out to be from the great ones. Had they not investigated the way they did and expended effort and energy in finding out the truth, the case would have remained a mystery with the general public believing it to be a case of suicide, which it was not!

Einstein once said, "Imagination is more important than knowledge. Knowledge is limited; imagination encircles the world."

Some cases are easy while others are not. If the truth is not coming to you, you should go to it. This is what the worthy officers of the Haines City Police Department did when they carried out the investigation procedure brilliantly. It was them doing their duty that led to the arresting of Christopher Gamble. After all, it was his confession that started a chain reaction, resulting in the automatic solving of the case but the Detectives and officers had played their part well too.

"With foxes we must play the fox."

— *Dr. Thomas Fuller*

Chapter 6

Catching the Final Culprit — Charles Fowler! (2008)

"How to Commit the Perfect Murder" was an old game in heaven. I always chose the icicle: the weapon melts away."

> — *Alice Sebold, The Lovely Bones*

While choosing an invisible weapon might be a great way to commit the perfect crime, even that could be traceable if the people investigating the crime are determined enough. Officer Horner's murder had been carried out with his own weapon. What could have been a better choice of weapon? It was indeed a great way to mislead the police department, making them believe that it was a case of suicide. However, it was not what the truth really was and since truth has a way of coming out, the matter unraveled as well. The real culprit was bound to be caught and he was, but not easily.

Law Enforcement, up until now, had been successful in catching three Suspects who were involved in Officer Horner's murder case. These were the pawns that merely had been present at the time of the crime and the real murderer was still missing. Law Enforcement was now on the lookout for the man who had pulled the trigger and shot the bullet that had claimed the life of an honest and brilliant officer.

The situation had somewhat turned into one of the Agatha Christie's whodunit mystery. Catching the final culprit was more difficult than the previous ones. Even Gamble had not given his name right away and it was only after the arrest of Robert Earl Winston that the fourth and final player in this murder mystery was to be caught. Yet the Investigators of the Polk County's Sheriff's Office were not easily deterred. They had known there was a fourth person behind the murder and he was yet to be caught.

The interesting point in this case is the dedication and commitment exhibited by the law enforcement personnel. The public is always skeptical of the efforts made by Law

Enforcement in regulating the law and catching criminals. This case, however, was one of the several other situations where the police had performed their duties in the best possible way.

As Sally Yates had once said, "It's really important to me that the public have confidence in their criminal justice system. We don't operate very well if the public doesn't trust us."

However, it is true that not all criminals are redemptive and not a single person should ever be considered above the law. If a crime has been committed, the balance of nature will only be restored if a suitable punishment is given to the criminal. This is the reason why irrespective of the countless appeals made by criminals in Officer Horner's case, they were denied the privileges they were asking for, as only the people who are truly repentant should be facilitated.

Murder is a capital crime and such felons must be punished according to their crime. Charles Fowler belongs to the second category of criminals as well. He needed to be put behind bars for his atrocities against the law and humanity. Taking a person's life just to save yourself is indeed a heartless crime. No wonder it is called murder in cold blood and this was what Charles Fowler had done. Thus, punishing him was crucial in order to save the integrity of humanity in general.

Did you know?

In March of 2016, on the 18th anniversary of the shooting of Officer Christopher Horner, the road leading to the Haines City Police Department was renamed as Officer Horner Memorial Lane. It was previously called West Johnson Avenue.

According to the Haines City Manager Jonathan Evans, the sign was put in a different color, allowing people to remember him and his sacrifice. He further added that any new recruit in the Police department would be asked about why the sign is in a different color and they would be told about the sacrifice made by Officer Christopher Todd Horner. After all, this is the least that could be done to honor the memory of those who make a sacrifice just to make this country great.

Jennifer Hall, the daughter of the deceased, was also attending the ceremony. She had been only 9 years old when she and her brother had learned that their father had been shot at the back of his head and was never going to return to them.

At the ceremony, she said that it was nice to know that there were other people who remembered her father as well. She said that it was unbelievable that her father was held in such high esteem.

A former Deputy Sheriff, Commissioner Roy Tyler was also present at the ceremony and said that it seemed like only a few years had passed since the unfortunate incident had happened. He said that this profession was perhaps the only one where you woke up each morning not knowing whether you would be able to return home or not. He further said that it was an honor to work in this profession but it may not always be a pleasure.

Charles Fowler and the Murder of Officer Horner

Charles Andrew Fowler was 25 years old when he was brought in for his trial. The infamous criminal had a series of crimes to his credit including several cases of robberies and drug dealing activities. He was a regular user of cocaine and was often associated with reckless behavior. He was Winston's cousin and along with their other friends, the two of them had committed a number of crimes.

Charles Fowler's name had come up in the investigations of Officer Horner's murder when Christopher Gamble decided to give his testimony where he had pleaded guilty. Gamble had admitted to conducting an armed robbery at a Holiday Inn and he also admitted to being a part of the gang that had murdered Officer Horner when he had cornered them at the Oakland Cemetery. According to the version of events narrated by him, there was only one man who had actually fired the shot while the rest of them had helped along and it was Charles Andrew Fowler.

It was a matter of preventing the officer from communicating with his dispatch operator at the station and thus getting away from the crime they had just committed. Apparently, the Officer recognized Gamble from the previous robbery cases he had been detained for and called him by his name.

"Why are you doing this, Chris?"

These words turned out to be his undoing for
when he uttered them; the Actors realized that
there was no walking back from the mess for
them. This was the moment when Fowler
decided to end the life of a hardworking and
honest officer. He committed cold blooded
murder.

*"Even those who want to go to heaven would
rather kill than be killed."*

— *MokokomaMokhonoana*

It was probably a case of do or die for him and
thus he decided to Do instead of being arrested
for his crimes. Going to heaven was definitely
not among his priorities but staying out of jail

was. The group tucked the Semi-Automatic Pistol under the body of Officer Horner. They were aiming to stage it as a suicide, which had worked for a while but Fowler was not to have it all that easily and thus Gamble did it for him.

Gamble was arrested in 2002 for his involvement in an armed robbery. As it so happened, Andrew Fowler had been indicted after a few hours of Gamble's arrest as well. According to the sources, his polygraph test concerning his involvement with Officer Horner's murder indicated that he was not being completely truthful on the matter when he claimed to have nothing to do with the Officer's murder.

The evidence provided by Gamble on the matter were in fact, of utmost importance and seemed to have a lot of truth in them. Gamble had clearly fingered Fowler to be the shooter but the police did not have enough evidence to arrest him.

Meanwhile, it had been a good 6 years since Officer Horner was first shot and his family was looking for some kind of closure. Thus, Gamble's confession had brought hope for them in a way nothing else would. Everyone in Officer Horner's Family and at his Police Department knew that this was not a case of suicide.

Haines City Police Chief Morris West applauded the development in Federal Court, calling it good news for Horner's family and his family of officers looking for closure in the 6-year-old case. Officer Horner was 35 years old when he was shot. He had left behind a family to fend for itself. He had a son and a 9-year-old daughter who were naturally deeply affected by the incident. The killers had definitely not considered that before pulling the trigger. Most crimes are like that after all! People are often unaware of the impact their actions could have in the long run. For Fowler, it was just a way out of a tight spot but in his act of selfishness, he had destroyed a young and happy family that probably had a lot of good times to look forward to in the future. Yet, he deprived them of it.

Kismet, however, was on the side of the righteous and Gamble's confession turned out to be the key that unlocked this long unsolved case. Catching Fowler turned out to be an easy job. He was often found at a certain spot in the streets and when the police went to arrest him, he was perched there as usual. They arrested him and he went with them without much struggle. For some reason, he was convinced that he would be out and about in a few hours' time. However, Law Enforcement had done their homework well this time.

The next day, the newspaper as well as the internet was abuzz with the news of this new development in the old case. For those who had been following the case of Polk County's Rookie, it was a big day. There was a general wave of excitement and people had their own speculations to make. While some believed that he would get away, there were others who trusted their criminal justice system.

As Ben Wishaw once said, "The criminal justice system, like any system designed by human beings, clearly has its flaws" but there are a number of things that are right in it too. It was in fact all that is right in our justice system that ensured justice was served. As Tray Gowdy had rightly said, "The reason I like the criminal justice system is there aren't Republican or Democrat victims or police officers or prosecutors. It's about respect for the rule of law!"

Charles Fowler had a history of violence and armed robberies. The investigation team at the Polk County's Sheriff Office did their investigation in detail. Their aim was to serve justice to a fallen Officer and thus, they delivered it too. Detective Giampavolo has a special role to play in this regard. The man had served the office from 2000 to 2005 at the Homicide Bureau and had been a great asset to the department. His achievements are numerous and this case was indeed the pinnacle of his great investigation skills. His team proved to be a group of experts who knew exactly how to go about their business. While Gamble's confession turned out to be one lucky break for them, they had not given up on the case even before it. That says something about their commitment and conviction!

Fowler, on the other hand, was sure that he was safe. He must have imagined that no harm was to come to him since he had not made any attempts to hide or go underground for that matter. In fact, when Gamble told the law Enforcement that he was ready to stand as a witness against his former partner in crime, Fowler, the latter did not try to run away.

The Police had other evidence that could be used against him and thus an arrest warrant was issued for the final culprit in the Officer Horner case. They were definitely expecting resistance and some kind of trouble from his side but surprisingly there was none. He was found sitting at his usual spot and came with the police rather quietly. The only point where he showed any sign of resistance was when the news reporters had tried to talk him as he was being arrested. Instead of giving them any answers, he had remained quiet but expressed his emotions by making obscene gestures at the camera while the whole world had its eyes fixed on him. However, that was it; he had come with the authorities without much struggle.

He started his resistance after being arrested. As it turned out, Fowler was a man of resources and he was planning to fight the Law by all means possible. Clinging to the claim of innocence, he was adamant on his stance — I have not murdered Officer Christopher Horner.

The law gives everyone, even criminals, the right to defend themselves. Therefore, Fowler decided to do just that and made an appeal to the court.

A criminal trial is never about seeking justice for the victim. If it were, there could be only one verdict: guilty.

— Alan Dershowitz

Appeal and conviction (2010 and 2011)

We live in a society where it is cool to be criminal.

— *Kurt Elling*

As we have established by now that Fowler was arrested on the pretext of violating the federal witness tampering statute. According to this statute, it is a crime that allows the law to subject the doer with appropriate punishment to kill someone in order to prevent them from communicating with the Federal Law Enforcement Office, thus stopping them from informing the concerned authorities about a possible commission of a Federal offence.

Since Fowler was being accused of committing just that, he went for an appeal. In his appeal, he argued that there was not sufficient evidence to prove that he had indeed killed Officer Horner with any intent to prevent the officer from establishing a contact with a federal officer relaying to him the possibility of commission of federal offence.

After the initial process got streamlined, the case finally reached the Supreme Court. The Eleventh Circuit, however, held the opinion that the evidence was indeed sufficient of the prosecutor to demonstrate a potential or possible communication of the victim with the federal authorities.

The case had went on for a while, during which Fowler tried his best to cheat the law and get away from the capital punishment or even life imprisonment. The court issued another interesting statement that emphasized that concerning the said circumstance, no state of mind need be proved that this judge is the judge of the United States and that the law enforcement officer is an employee of the Federal Government.

This statement in addition to the first one allowed the court to draw the following two logical conclusions that when having to prosecute a case like this one, the Government should prove:

1. An attempt at killing or a killing

2. That was committed with a certain

   intent such as an intent to

   a. prevent a communication

   b. regarding the possible

      commission or actual

      commission of a Federal

      offense

   c. reported to a federal judge

      or law enforcement officer

When all of the above pointers were combined,

the court succeeded at creating the following

question concerning the said appeal:

How the appeal statement applies if the

defendant (1) killed a victim with an (2) intent

to prevent the (a) communication (b) about the possible commission or the commission of a federal offence (c) to a law enforcement officials in general instead of any particular law enforcement officer or a group of officers that the defendant had in mind.

Therefore, you see, concerning Fowler's appeal, the question that rose in the minds of the judiciary was that if Fowler had some particular person in mind that he feared the victim would communicate to when he killed him.

Fowler v. United States

In order to give our readers a detailed insight into the matters, we have surmised the court proceedings. Following are the details crucial to understand the nature of Fowler's appeal.

1. Fowler was consistent in his statement that the court had failed to bring to light any concrete evidence that Officer Horner would have eventually contacted federal officers to report Fowler's previous crimes if he was not killed. This absence of evidence, according to Fowler and his attorney, meant that his prosecution under the 18 U.S.C. § 1512(a)(1)(C) was not justified. Moreover, they argued that in such circumstances, adoption of the Eleventh Circuit's interpretation of the particular statute was inconsistent with

the intent with which the Congress had

passed the statute. Therefore, such as

statement would end up raising

federalism concerns.

2. On the contrary, the Respondent, the

    United States, argued that a logical

    likelihood of communication between

    the murdered officer and the federal

    authorities was sufficient to convict the

    murderer under the statute. The

    government argued that if asked for a

    higher showing, the statute's target of

    protecting the integrity of the federal

    justice system would not be achieved.

The government further argued that the

Eleventh Circuit's interpretation of the statute

was originally designed as a part of the <u>Victim and Witness Protection Act of 1982</u>, in order to avoid the loss of evidence, which often happened when the witnesses to federal crimes were murdered all the time for ensuring the prevention of their communicating the truth to the responsible federal authorities. The argument made by the United States further stated that if the Court was to accept Fowler's interpretation of the statute, it would become extremely difficult for the federal prosecutors to be able to convict the individuals responsible for a crime under the Section 1512(a)(1)(C). Therefore, the statement continued, the Congress's intention to guard the sanctity of the federal justice system would be undermined.

The State-Federal Balance — Fowler's Appeal

Are you as much of a criminal if you do not act when there is a crime, taking place in front of you as you are one of the participants? That was something that I was thinking about a lot because there are many moments in 'Less Than Zero' where horrific things happen and Clay could do something about them, but his passivity stops him.

— Bret Easton Ellis

Fowler's appeal was basically based on the premises that allowing this case under the jurisdiction of the federal justice system was likely to disturb the State-Federal balance. According to him, the government's decision of convicting murders under the Eleventh Circuit statute rule without providing sufficient proof that the murdered victim would have contacted the federal authorities, expands the federal criminal jurisdiction to the territory, which should be reserved for the state law solely. He was talking about the crime of murder there.

His statement further threw light on the point stating that the federal government has the authority to deal with murders only if they are touching the federal interest. Allowing Federal jurisdiction to interfere on the premises that the victim might have contacted the said authorities should not be allowed, as it does not justify its connection to the federal authorities. Fowler said he believed that this would hurt the sanctity of the law, as the state-federal balance would be threatened.

The United States counter-argued his statement. The government stated that affirmation of the Eleventh Circuit's decision would not modify or disturb the state-federal balance in any way. The government further contended that the purpose of the concerned statute was to ensure that the integrity of the federal criminal justice system was preserved. Moreover, it stated that the Congress had the authority to punish crimes that compromised this integrity. Since killing individuals who are witnesses to federal crimes compromises the sanctity of the federal criminal justice system, the federal government had the right to punish such crime, even if the possibility that the murdered victim would have contacted the federal authorities is not conclusive and only reasonable given the particular circumstances. Therefore, the United States content adoption of the Eleventh Circuit's reading of the decree, was not disrupting the spirit of <u>federalism</u> in any way.

Analysis of the Court's Proceedings

The summary of the Fowler case was that he was found guilty of murder by a jury under the section <u>18 U.S.C. § 1512(a)(1)(C)</u>, which deals with homicides committed with the intention of delaying or preventing the communication of crucial information regarding a federal offense between a witness and a federal law enforcement officer.

Charles Fowler decided not to accept the decision as it was and made an appeal against it. He argued that the government did not have enough evidence to prove that had he not murdered Officer Horner, the victim would have communicated with the federal officer. Therefore, this was not a federal crime in his opinion and should not be dealt as such either.

To his appeal, the government answered with the Eleventh Circuit that decided to upheld his conviction given the argument that the evidence just had to demonstrate that this communication was indeed a possibility.

Finally, it turned out to be the responsibility of the <u>Supreme Court of the United States</u> to address whether the possibility level for the certainty was appropriate, making the evidence concrete enough to make the jury's decision of finding Fowler guilty appropriate.

Lawyers claim that their clients have been grossly mistreated, which is what criminal defense lawyers are paid to do.

— Ken Starr

Eleventh Circuit's Interpretation — the Statute's level of certainty requirement

In this case, both parties came to an agreement that giving a mere remote possibility or a theoretical idea that the murder was responsible for preventing the communication of information between the federal officers and the victim was insufficient. However, their disagreement was about how much higher that standard should be?

The Statute's language was of not much assistance in this matter since it was silent on this particular topic.

Fowler or his representative attorney was of the opinion that the Eleventh Circuit was in error since it considered the mere possibility of communication by the victim sufficient to make it a federal crime irrespective of who the receiver of that information was.

He argued that accepting this state of affairs would relinquish the difference between communicating to the state or to the federal officers. This would in turn render the situation superfluous. Moreover, he contended that if the mere possibility would have sufficed as a condition to make it a federal crime, the statute would have said so. On the contrary, the statute had not used words such as possibility or likelihood. Therefore, for the crime to come under the federal jurisdiction, it must have had sufficient proof that the dying man would have certainly communicated with the federal law enforcement officer(s) but there is no certainty in this situation.

The United States continued to defend the Eleventh Circuit's interpretation where it was adamant on the "reasonable possibility" being enough of evidence. They argued that in any criminal trial, the evidence should form a reasonable basis to reach any conclusive inference that the jury might make.

Therefore, the government disagreed to Fowler's point and stated that the Eleventh Circuit's interpretation fulfilled the requirement of a reasonable possibility of there being a federal correspondence. Moreover, it said that as per this reading, there is a distinction between a local and a federal officer. Therefore, the government must present evidence to conclude that there had been a reasonable possibility of the homicide being prevented had there been communication between the victim and the federal officials.

Then Fowler kept on countering the arguments provided by the government while the government stood ground as the proceeding of the court continued. After several arguments and counter arguments, the final verdict came that the lack of concrete proof that Officer Horner would have communicated with the

Federal law enforcement officers, did not threaten the federal-state balance. This was a defining moment in the case because this meant that the jury was not wrong in finding Fowler guilty. However, this would have the ultimate conclusion but the immediate one stated that the federalism was not threatened by this decision.

To count or not to count

The Federal Law originally sentenced Fowler for two counts in 2008. The first count stated that he had murdered Officer Horner in order to prevent him from making contact with a federal official. This first count came under the federal witness-tampering section and was considered as a federal offence. As per count 2, Fowler was charged with the offence of using a firearm in a federal crime of violence — with the initial intent of committing bank robbery that led to the shooting of the officer. The Federal court found the accused guilty on both accounts.

This led to Fowler's appeal in the court with the main concerns that this was not a federal crime in the first place because there was not sufficient proof that Officer Horner would have communicated with a federal official. The courts had sentenced the culprit to life imprisonment and an additional 10 years' Imprisonment for both the counts. The court proceedings took around 5 years in coming up with their final verdict.

Fowler was adamant that the witness-tampering part was not true. Thus, the case was brought forward to the Supreme Court. The court granted that the government should have something more to show than just the possibility of the aforementioned communication. The Court maintained that the government should at least establish reasonable likelihood that the deceased would have made one relevant communication at the least. The Supreme Court than forwarded the case to the district court on remand.

The district court thus concluded that the evidence provided by the government was insufficient and unable to satisfy the standards set by the Supreme Court. However, it allowed the government to retry the accused on Count 1. The government informed the district court that they were not interested in pursuing a retrial on count 1.

The district court judge also said that whether there would be a trial by the government or not, the sentence on count 2 would be vacated because it was announced in addition to count 1 and if that was not to be held, the other count should be vacated too. There was no way anybody with a murder-with-a-firearm charge would be sentenced to ten years. The judge had obviously sentenced for count 2 in addition to the life imprisonment that was sentenced for Count 1.

Since the government refused the opportunity to retry Fowler on Count 1, the court decided to vacate Fowler's conviction and the consequent life sentence on that count as well as the consecutive sentence of 10 years for Count 2. Moreover, the court decided to retry Fowler for Count 2.

Resentencing of life imprisonment (November 01, 2012)

At the district court's direction, the probation office prepared an updated PSR calculating the applicable guidelines range on the sole surviving count of conviction. Even without his conviction on Count 1, Fowler's total offense level on

Count 2 remained at 46, his criminal history category remained at VI, and the sentence recommended by the guidelines remained at life imprisonment, the statutory maximum for that offense under 18 U.S.C. § 924(j)(1). Fowler did not object to the PSR's revised guidelines calculations; instead, he objected to the resentencing process in general.

Fowler insisted that the district court lacked the authority to resentence him under the so-called "sentencing package doctrine" because his two original counts of conviction were not "interdependent" for sentencing purposes. He argued that those two counts were not interdependent because Count 2 "was not predicated on the [witness-tampering] offense alleged in Count 1" and the two counts had not

been grouped together in the PSR calculations

for the original sentencing. Fowler alternatively

argued that, even if the district court could

proceed with resentencing, it could not impose

a sentence greater than the ten-year term

originally imposed on Count 2 without raising a

presumption of judicial vindictiveness. That

presumption, he asserted, was not one the

government could overcome.

The District Court further determined that the

authority to resentence Fowler on Count 2

belonged to them since the previous sentences

for Count 1 and Count 2 was a package and the

sentence for the second Count was indeed

based on Count 1. Moreover, the Court further

explained that both the sentences were not only related on the basis of their factuality, stemming from the same cause that was Officer Horner's murder, but that they also had structural similarity, since Count 2's sentence was consecutive to the sentence that had been imposed for the first Count.

The government then argued and insisted on sentencing him with life imprisonment for Count 2 because of several reasons such as the brutal and senseless nature of the crime, the guidelines recommended for the said crime, and the extensive criminal history of Fowler. Using these factors as the guideline, the district court pronounced its verdict on the resentencing of Fowler for Count 2. The Count

resentenced him for life imprisonment for
Count 2.

Fowler had a Foul Stance

Fowler had a contention with respect to the
decision made by the court. He maintained that
the district court did not have the authority to
resentence him on the surviving count of
conviction that was Count 2. According to him,
the original 10-year sentence should have
sufficed. In order to counter the "sentencing
doctrine package", he further argued that the
firearm count was not in any way
interdependent with the witness tampering
charge. Also, he pointed out that the two
charges have not been grouped together as per

the sentencing guidelines mentioned in the PSR for the original sentencing.

The "sentencing package doctrine" label should be considered a misnomer since it is not really a doctrine but more of a common judicial practice that is grounded as a basic notion of the sentencing decision guide especially for cases involving multiple counts.

This notion states, especially in the guidelines era, that sentencing for multiple counts is an interconnected, interrelated, and holistic process that requires a court for the crafting of an overall sentence (called the sentence package), which shows the specific guidelines and applicable § 3553(a) factors.

On the other hand, the government and the district court maintained that in a multi-count case, a criminal sentence, by its nature, is "a package of sanctions utilized by the district court to effectuate its sentencing intent making it consistent with the Sentencing Guidelines" as well as with the § 3553(a) factors. The philosophy behind this rule is that when there is a conviction and either one or more of the counts are to be vacated for good; the district court has complete right to reconstruct the sentencing package. This is essential in order to make sure that the overall sentence stays in accordance with the court's verdict, the § 3553(a) factors, and with the concerned guidelines.

While the government and the district courts were clear on their stance of resentencing Fowler for his convictions, he was persistent on his claim. He was basing his challenge on the supposition that there was no interdependence between the two counts for which he was sentenced earlier. This thinking procedure is basically based on an outdated distinction between resentencing processes right after a successful direct appeal for those that follow a successful 28 U.S.C. § 2255 proceeding.

When the direct appeal was registered, the court had routinely, without any hesitation, as a matter of course, vacated the entire sentences. Moreover, they remanded for the resentencing on all the remaining counts after they have vacated a conviction or sentence on a part of it, but not all, of the counts.

As it had been studied and discussed in detail, in the situation where the trial judge is presented with a number of count convictions, they are required to come up with a sentencing scheme that would take into consideration the entire offence in relation to the defendant's behavior. Now the legislative rules further state that if there is a disruption in this sentence or in the part of the sentence because it might have incorporated an illegal portion, then it is only essential to remand the entire case for resentencing. This has been the practice of most of the judges and is considered the most correct way to go about the business if such a situation arises.

On the other hand, if the convictions are set aside in the § 2255 proceedings, the judges' willingness to allow full resentencing on counts that were unchallenged was at a time more limited. It was in the pre-guidelines era that they believed it to be an improper practice to resentence a defendant on the other counts remaining after one of the counts was set aside in a § 2255 proceeding.

However, when in 1987, the sentencing guidelines were promulgated, they changed course. They decided to hold that with the guidelines sentences where some of the counts of conviction were set aside in a § 2255

proceeding, the district court retains the

authority of resentencing the defendant for the

counts of conviction that were left behind. Yet,

in such a situation, it would be essential that

such counts were "interdependent" with the

counts that were aside. This would result in

what is termed as "an aggregate sentence." This

term was probably a collateral replacement for

"sentence package."

This requirement of interdependence for

allowing resentencing of a count after that

conviction had been vacated in a § 2255

proceeding was then seen as nothing, but was

just like the requirement for resentencing after

the conviction had been vacated on a direct appeal.

Fowler was only trying to manipulate the law in his favor. It was his attempt to run away from the punishment he deserved for murdering an officer of Horner's caliber. 10 years of jail is after all, a small price to pay for taking someone's life. The court, however, was not to be so easily manipulated. They maintained the stance that as long as the district court "viewed the defendant's original sentence as a 'package,'" the counts of conviction and the parts of the sentences ensuing from them would be interdependent enough for the district court to allow it to revisit them even after one of the components is set aside.

Human progress is neither automatic

nor inevitable... Every step toward the

goal of justice requires sacrifice,

suffering, and struggle; the tireless

exertions and passionate concern of

dedicated individuals.

— *Martin Luther King, Jr.*

The district court had previously brought to

them cases like these. The court stood

confident in its decision regarding the

unbundling of the sentence. However, in this

case, the unbundling occurred after Fowler

made a direct appeal. In making this appeal, he

was adhering to the rules belonging to a bygone

era. One point of his argument stated that since

he had made the direct appeal according to the § 2255 proceedings, Count 1 of his conviction would have been set aside too. The Court, however, believed that it did not matter if the Count 1 charges were set aside because of his direct appeal or the § 2255 proceedings, since there was no difference in either case as per the post-guidelines era.

The judge presiding over the case said that in such a situation, the court—of pre-guidelines as well as post-guidelines era—has always believed that the sentences on every component of a multi-count conviction make an entire package that can be revisited without following any further case inquiry. This is to make sure that the overall sentence on the

remaining counts follows the intentions of the
district court, the guidelines dictating the
decisions, and the § 3553(a) factors.

The judge further explained that this is for the
cases where the jury would reach the same
conclusion with or without following any case
specific inquiry. Moreover, the district court
made it clear, even though it was not a
requirement for them to do so, that when
Fowler had been sentenced the first time, the
court had viewed the sentence it had imposed
on him as 'a package sentence.' Besides this,
the language of the sentence for Count 2 was
self-evident in the way that it could not be used
independently. It said, "10 years of consecutive
imprisonment" and by setting aside Count 1,

there was no sentence consecutive with the Count 2 sentence that could be implemented. According to the rules of the court, for a conviction whose sentence structure has been dismantled because a part of it has been vacated, the district court holds the right to redesign and rebuild it in order to achieve the purpose of conforming to the code and ensuring that justice is served. The package was now to be repackaged in order to ensure that the punishment would fit the criminal as well as the crime.

Fowler was relying on an outdated rule and there were three major reasons because of which his reliance was misplaced. First of all, in the case of Monaco did not prohibit, categorically, the district court from impressing a longer or more severe sentence for resentencing. Secondly, the pre-guideline approach that was previously given by Monaco for determining the severity of a new sentence in relation to an older one, also called the aggregate remainder approach, was not applicable in the post-guideline era. Moreover, it presented a significantly difference situation that the one that involved this case.

Moreover, even if the pre-guidelines of Monaco were to be extended to the post-guidelines era, it would not have affected the result of this case since the life sentence that the district court imposed for Count 2 was supported and appeared in the record as non-vindictive reasons.

I think the first duty of society is justice.

— Alexander Hamilton

Three Reasons why Monaco Wouldn't be Applicable to Fowler's case

Fowler and his attorney were adamant that Monaco should be extended to their case, and believed that the Pearce rule applied to their situation. Here are the aforementioned reasons discussed in detail to show why Monaco and the Pearce rule did not apply to Fowler's case:

1. The constitutional rule applied by Monaco was first articulated in North Carolina v. Pearce, 395 U.S. 711, 89 S.Ct. 2072 (1969). According to this articulation, it was held by the Supreme Court in Pearce that 'there would be absolutely no constitutional bar if the court believes that a more severe sentence should be imposed upon retrial or upon resentencing.' However, the due process would require that vindictiveness against the defendant for attacking and successfully defending his first conviction should not play any part in the determining of the next sentence that he would receive. 395 U.S. at 723–

25, 89 S.Ct. at 2080. Pearce adopted a prophylactic rule for controlling the risk of resentencing based on vindictiveness. According to this rule, there are two conditions under which the presumption of vindictiveness might arise: (i) if the resentencing judge decides to impose a more severe sentence (ii) there are no non-vindictive reasons of doing that and it does not "affirmatively appear" to be because of a non-vindictive reason in the record.7 Id. at 726, 89 S.Ct. at 2081; see also Alabama v. Smith, 490 U.S. 794, 798, 109 S.Ct. 2201, 2204 (1989).

In case these two conditions are present, "a presumption can arise that [the] more severe sentence was imposed for a vindictive purpose. In order to justify the increase in sentence, objective justification should be used to rebut this presumption". Smith, 490 U.S. at 798–99, 109 S.Ct. at 2204.

Considering the above logic, we can conclude that contrary to the suggestion made by Fowler, the Monaco decision was not in contradiction to the Pearce rule for categorically barring the court from deciding on a greater sentence upon resentencing. This is because according to that, the Pearce rule would have been violated if the trial judge had failed to affirmatively state the reasons behind the said increase. Monaco, 702 F.2d at 885. In this case, as we will explain later, the district court did affirmatively state the reasons for the increased sentence on Count 2. See infra Part III. C.

2. The part that Monaco really added to Pearce was about devising the particular method to determine if the new sentence in a multi-count case was actually an increase over the previous one or not. If that is not the case, then

there is no reason to raise an appeal or request an investigation since Pearce would not apply in this case. See Monaco, 702 F.2d at 885. In the case of Monaco, the defendant had been convicted on three Counts. He was sentenced for them with consecutive time in prison of two years, one year, and one year respectively. Id. at 883. The defendant made an appeal and was given a retrial. This led to the dismissal of the third count for the lack of sufficient evidence.

The district court later granted a new trial and, upon retrial, dismissed the third count due to insufficient evidence.

However, when the jury convicted the defendant of the remaining two trials, the court sentenced them to serve consecutive four years of imprisonment, two on each count. While this meant that the total years of imprisonment were the same, the authorities concluded that the Pearce rule applied to this situation. This is because when checking the two sentences against each other, the aggregate remainder of the imprisonment terms is compared for only the remaining counts. Id. at 885; see also United States v. Campbell, 106 F.3d 64, 67–68 (5th Cir.1997).Since in this case, the aggregate sentence for

the two remaining counts of the

defendant had increased, the court

drew the conclusion that the Pearce

rule applied. Monaco, 702 F.2d at 885.

If this aggregate remainder approach

was to be used, Fowler's resentencing

of life imprisonment compared to the

original sentence of ten years for the

second count would have been

considered as severe. However, the

court, here, had used the aggregate

package approach. See Campbell, 106

F.3d at 67–68. According to this second

approach, the aggregate of the original

sentence, which was in this case life

imprisonment with consecutive 10 years, was compared with the new sentence after retrial, which was life sentence. Therefore, Pearce would not be applicable to this situation.

Also, Monaco arose prior to the guidelines era and the guidelines changed a lot of rules and the method of sentencing, especially for the federal judiciary structure. While the aggregate remainder approach of Monaco could be used for circumstances and the evidence that are rather similar to the ones during which it arose, the court was under no obligation to extend that decision to a situation that differed from this one considerably. Anders, 346

F.3d at 1031; see also Dantzler v. I.R.S.,

183 F.3d 1247, 1251 (11th Cir.1999).

After all, the law states that there is a

considerable difference between

following a precedent where it is a

requirement and extending a precedent

without any obligation to do so.

Monaco had surfaced in1983. At that

time, the district courts had the

freedom to exercise a discretion, which

could be called almost unfettered in

imposing sentences for those who had

been accused of committing federal

offences. It was subjected to almost

none appellate review, as long as those

sentences were within the statutory boundaries, which were set by Congress and were considered as "customarily wide". See Tapia v. United States, —— U.S. ——, 131 S.Ct. 2382, 2386–87 (2011) (quotation marks omitted); see also United States v. Irey, 612 F.3d 1160, 1180 (11th Cir.2010) (en banc). In short, it can be said that before there were any sentencing guidelines for the federal judiciary structure, the district courts had the "unbridled discretion" to pass any sentence they liked and the only boundaries they had to keep themselves from crossing were rather broad ones set by Congress. When it came to exercising that power, the judge had the authority to conduct a broad-scoped inquiry, which was mostly unlimited to the type and source of information. United States v. Tucker, 404 U.S. 443, 446, 92 S.Ct. 589, 591 (1972). This was how the sentencing procedure worked in the pre-guidelines era.

Thus, a need to revise such laws was felt and this is how the Sentencing Reform Act, 1984, dramatically changed the landscape of federal sentencing. This rule channeled the discretion process of sentencing judges and established the sentencing guidelines, by indicating certain factors that should be considered for the effective sentencing procedure. See Tapia, 131 S.Ct. at 2387–88; 18 U.S.C. § 3553; see also Irey, 612 F.3d at 1181. The post guidelines were therefore subjected to sufficient scrutiny as compared to the pre-guidelines.

Considering the above facts and the previous cases, the court declined to extend the aggregate remainder approach of Monaco to Fowler's case. The Supreme Court maintained that it had been clearly established that the Pearce Court's primary concern was to prevent vindictive sentencing procedures and there was no need to extend it to the "increase in sentence pertaining to a valid reason" where there is no proof that it had been done for vindictiveness. Smith, 490 U.S. at 799, 109 S.Ct. at 2204–05.

Moreover, while in the post guideline era, it was understandable and was considered defensible to make an appeal if the sentence on retrial was increased, as it could be because of vindictiveness on the judge's part. The post-guideline era, however, had no room for that thought.

Further evidence that the resentencing of life imprisonment to Fowler was not against the law but exactly according to it can be discovered by studying his case. While his successful challenge on the count stripped away his original life sentence, leaving him with only the consecutive 10-year sentence on Count 2, his crime was still very much there that needed sentencing. His advisory sentence, according to the guidelines era alone, was life imprisonment. See Peugh, 133 S.Ct. at 2083–84. The binding guidelines commentary states unequivocally that in case of premeditated killing, the criminal should serve a life sentence if sentence of death has not been imposed. U.S.S.G.

§ 2A1.1 cmt. 2(A); see also United

States v. Wilks, 464 F.3d 1240, 1245

(11th Cir.2006).

However, if Monaco's rule of aggregate

remainder was to be applied to it, any

sentencing above ten years on Count 2

would have taken it to the realm of

"vindictive sentencing". On the other

hand, a ten year sentence for a murder

would have been a huge variance from

the range of guidelines that it would

certainly be unreasonable under the §

3553(a) factors. See Gall, 552 U.S. at 50,

128 S.Ct. at 597.

3. There is a third reason why Fowler's

claim for implying the Pearce claim

should not work. Let's suppose, for the purpose of understanding the situation, that Monaco's aggregate remainder could be extended to Fowler's resentencing, only the first predicament of the presumption of vindictiveness existed but the second didn't. For that presumption to hold true, the second predicament was that the reasons of the increase in the sentences did not appear in the record representing the resentencing. Pearce, 395 U.S. at 726, 89 S.Ct. at 2081; see also Smith, 490 U.S. at 798, 109 S.Ct. at 2204.

In Fowler's case, the record of his resentencing had clearly written in it as to why the district court had resentenced him life imprisonment for Count 2. It was right according to the law since not only the § 3553 factors were in support of it, but the guidelines' range, calculated by the court and in the PSR, recommended a life sentence. See United States v. Eldick, 443 F.3d 783, 790 (11th Cir.2006). In addition to that, the district court had explained affirmatively that a life sentence was imposed because the original separate sentences on Count 1 and Count 2 were considered to be a package sentence. It was clearly stated that the court would not have decided on a 10 year sentence if there had not been a life sentence on Count 1 already. The life sentence was essential in the court's opinion considering the seriousness of the defendant's offence as well as his extensive criminal background. See McCullough, 475 U.S. at 140, 106 S.Ct. at 980.

Serving justice was essential in this case as well as it would have been in any other. Letting the criminal go without appropriate punishment for his offence would have meant that injustice was being done to Officer Christopher Horner, to his family that needed closure, and to his memory. As Martin Luther King, Jr. said, "injustice anywhere is a threat to justice everywhere".

On Officer Horner's murder case, the court made the following two points of arguments when announcing their decision on the resentencing for Andrew Fowler:

- The district court had the power to resentence the defendant on Count 2 after the reversal of the conviction on Count 1.

- The life imprisonment sentence imposed on him for the remaining Count was neither a result of vindictiveness nor was it more severe than the total of his original sentence

Considering the arguments presented above, the presiding judges for the resentencing for Fowler's crime affirmed the sentence of life imprisonment.

"Justice will not be served until those who are unaffected are as outraged as those who are."

—Benjamin Franklin

Chapter 8

Remorse and redemption — the story of Mr. Gamble

"Redemption is something you have to fight for in a very personal, down-dirty way. Some of our characters lose that, some stray from that, and some regain it."

— *Joss Whedon*

While Fowler was being sentenced and resentenced, there was another man sitting in a prison cell reflecting on his crimes and sins. Christopher Gamble is still considered to be among the top reasons why justice was served in Officer Horner's murder case. He was the one who had pleaded guilty in the first place. Moreover, he had the guts to narrate the details of the incident and even revealed the names of his other accomplices who were a part of the murder. It therefore, goes, to his credit that Fowler was finally brought to the court and despite his several tries to run away from justice, he was brought to court nevertheless. Gamble stood in the court every time he was called upon, as a witness in the case and he did not falter when it came to telling the truth even once. In fact, he was the one whose presence forced Andre T. Paige, another of the criminal/robber involved in the murder, to confess to the robbery, which further developed the case to the point where the evidence started to pour in. Therefore, it would not be wrong that in his own way, Christopher Gamble had contributed a lot to it and was the star of this case. After all, telling the truth and standing up against your friends requires a lot of courage on your part.

"It takes strength and courage to admit the truth."

— Rick Riordan, The Red Pyramid

When Christopher Gamble had pleaded guilty in Officer Horner's case, the majority of the concerned parties believed that he had done it to have his sentence reduced. However, when he had done so, he was to serve 12 years of sentence in jail for an armed robbery and his pleading guilty won him a life sentence plus 107 years of imprisonment. Therefore, the question arose as to why would he trade 12 years with life imprisonment. There were many who still doubted his motive and intentions. They stated that he had done it because the police were investing the case and he was a suspect already so he just gave in to the pressure. Very few people realized his true intentions. One way or another, he was remorseful for what he had done, and it was redemption that he sought when he confessed the truth to the law enforcement officials.

"Dread remorse when you are tempted to err, Miss Eyre; remorse is the poison of life."

— Charlotte Brontë, Jane Eyre

When the Victim's Family Interceded

In the same year that Andrew Fowler had been condemned for life imprisonment on the count of his role in the murder of the respected Officer Horner, the victim's family decided to intercede on Christopher Gamble's part.

The victim's family as well as the prosecutors spoke in Gamble's favor. They requested the judge to reduce his sentence while being in full knowledge of the part he had played in the slaying of their beloved Haines City police officer around 11 years ago. The family believed that it was because of this man that they had received some kind of closure. In a way, he had cleared the Officer's name who until now had been accused of committing suicide. It must have been hard for the family to cope with the death of their beloved but it must be worse to have no closure — not knowing what had actually happened with him.

To run away from trouble is a form of cowardice and, while it is true that the suicide braves death, he does it not for some noble object but to escape some ill.

— Aristotle

When this happened, most of the people felt that this would make Gamble happy as this was exactly what he had wanted in the first place. The fact of the matter was that they could not understand the reason why, all of a sudden, this man had decided to tell the truth and were, therefore, looking for some kind of validation to prove that evil never repents.

It is hard to believe that a man is telling the truth when you know that you would lie if you were in his place.

— H. L. Mencken

People had their speculations and imaginations were running wild on this one for sure. However, a strong shut up call was delivered to them when Christopher Gamble refused the offer. He told the judge that he was part of the heinous crime that was committed in the cemetery 11 years ago. Therefore, he deserved to spend the remaining years of his life behind bars for his actions.

When questioned about this, Gamble's lawyer said that he had never encountered anything like that in his life before. The prosecutors as well as the family of the slain Officer Horner were adamant that Gamble should be rewarded because if not for him, there was no chance that the case would ever have been solved. Therefore, they wanted to repay the gratitude they felt towards him in kindness.

Feeling gratitude and not expressing it is like wrapping a present and not giving it.

— William Arthur Ward

An Appeal to have his sentence reduced

James Muench — Assistant U.S. Attorney— asked the judge presiding over the case to reduce Gamble's sentence from life imprisonment plus 107 years in the federal prison to a tenure of 24 years behind bars. In order to reinforce his request, the Assistant Attorney also read a letter to the judge, which was written by Jennifer — Horner's daughter, who was 9 years old when her father had been murdered. We have copied it for the readers below:

"For 10 years I blamed myself. I blamed myself because I did not know whom else to blame. After reading Christopher Gamble's testimony, I realized my father's life made a difference for him. I do not feel that there will ever be closure because nothing can bring my father back, but Christopher Gamble gave my family and me the second best thing — the truth. Chris, John 8:32 says, 'The truth shall set you free.' That quote is applicable to my life 100 percent, and I hope through this resentencing, it will be applicable to yours as well."

'Beauty is truth, truth beauty,' - that is all ye know on earth, and all ye need to know.

— John Keats

This was a beautiful letter that showed that she had indeed forgiven Gamble. His lawyer and public defender, Adam Allen further helped with the reduction of the sentence by reading the letter Chris had written to him around 4 years ago. In this letter, he had admitted that the reason behind his cooperation was indeed remorse for what he had done. He admitted that nightmares about what he had done haunted him. Therefore, he had realized that it was time for him to make things right. He wrote that he wished he had killed Charles Andrew Fowler, the man who killed Officer Todd Horner instead of letting him pull the trigger that released the fatal shot for the worthy Officer.

Adam Allen had also said that Christopher Gamble had even tried to interrupt him when he was making an appeal to James Moody — the U.S. District Judge — to reduce Gamble's sentencing, granting the prosecutor's motion. However, Adam's attempt of ignoring him did not work because then Gamble decided to speak and made it clear that he did not want to have his sentence changed. He said that he deserved to spend the rest of his life rotting in prison. All he had wanted was to bring the other culprits to justice as well. This was the way he would be able to face the family of the person they had participated in murdering.

Three things cannot be long hidden: the sun, the moon, and the truth.

— Buddha

When Allen was asked about it, he said that he had no idea that Gamble was going to do what he had done. However, he continued his statement claiming that even though he had no prior idea about it, he was not particularly shocked. "Knowing Christopher Gamble", he had said, "It was not a surprise at all." From day 1, the whole affair had not been about reducing his sentence or getting himself out of jail for him. Allen believed that it were the words of Officer Horner's daughter that had touched him truly. Her words somehow had more meaning for him than getting himself out of jail.

When we quit thinking primarily about ourselves and our own self-preservation, we undergo a truly heroic transformation of consciousness.

— Joseph Campbell

Moody further said that more often than not, prosecutors are the ones advocating for more severe sentences while the defendants look for easier sentences such as less time in jail. This time, however, the practice was surprisingly quite different. While the prosecution and the defendants were still not on the same side, it was the prosecution that was advocating for less time in jail and the defendant was disagreeing with the court's decision. When Christopher Gamble had said that he was not in favor of having his sentence reduced, the jury had something else in mind.

Therefore, it was not much of a surprise when the judge said, as they often do, in such situations, that he would be ignoring what the defendant had to say on the matter. He would make the just decision based on what is right and holds true to the spirit of the court and justice. However, he reserved the decision for a time, allowing the lawyers to discuss and give their opinions on what should be done next.

While the jury was busy making their decision, what needed to be appreciated was the beauty of transformation that a criminal had gone through. Being rigid about it and sticking to being stingy with someone who had sinned in the past but is now remorseful is not what justice should be. This is why the law was so anxious to compensate Gamble for his courage to stand against his friends in order to support and further the cause of justice. He had supported the law and now it was time for the law to pay him in kindness for his help.

Personal transformation can and does have global effects. As we go, so goes the world, for the world is us. The revolution that will save the world is ultimately a personal one.

— Marianne Williamson

Why was Gamble Important

Officer Horner was murdered in a cemetery. He was shot by his own firearm. In the history of Haines City, he was the first officer to be shot in the line of duty. The incident occurred in

1998 Various people kept on speculating that this was a case of suicide. Meanwhile, the family kept on suffering and his friends were baffled. They knew that it was highly unlikely that their friend would have committed suicide and this realization was obviously a heavy burden for them. For four years, there was no progress.

It was only in the year 2002 that the case was solved to some extent. This was all because of Christopher Gamble who decided to come forward and tell the truth in the hope that the truth would set him free of the ghosts that haunted him.

He admitted his role not just in the Holiday Inn robbery that had preceded the murder of Officer Horner but also in his murder. He informed the authorities about all the details on how he and his four other accomplices had jumped as the police officer had caught them as they were planning their next bank robbery in the cemetery.

When he was done telling them about his side of the story, the police asked him to meet his friends face to face and make them admit what they had done. However, not a single one of them had confessed to it. The best he got was Andre T. Paige admitting to the robbery part but even he did not admit murdering anyone.

Since none of them had confessed, the authorities decided to ask Gamble to testify against his friends in court. He did as he was told. There was nothing that could stop him from telling the truth now. He stood against every one of the culprits and ensured that justice was served.

"There are all kinds of courage. It takes a great deal of bravery to stand up to our enemies, but just as much to stand up to our friends".

— Albus Dumbledore, Harry Potter and the Sorcerer's Stone.

This led to the great breakthrough in the case. Andre T. Paige, Charles Fowler, and Robert Winston were tried and convicted at separate trials. The fifth man who had been there at the time of the slaying of the worthy officer, however, was not charged since he did not have a direct role to play in the murder. Standing against these criminals was not an easy task. Gamble was called a snitch and a liar. His intentions were questioned, and he was blamed of inventing lies to save his skin. However, he did not give ear to any of the propaganda that was being raised against him and continued to stick to his claims and was ready to testify against the criminals whenever the court asked him to. His testimonials kept on being agreed to by the courts as well. The case was finally moving towards its closure and at the end; it was only Christopher Gamble whose fate was to be decided. The prosecutions wanted to save him from the fate of life imprisonment, but he was after redemption and told the court that he deserved to serve the sentence.

Muench had written in his motion for reducing Christopher Gamble's sentence that if not for Gamble's testimony, three men involved in the execution of Officer Horner would have escaped prosecution and Officer Horner's children would have grown up wondering whether their father had taken his own life. Without Gamble, the government had nothing.